Ministry of LOVE

A Handbook for Visiting the Aged

Rev. Stephen V. Doughty

Ministry of LOVE

A Handbook for Visiting the Aged

Rev. Stephen V. Doughty

Ave Maria Press, Notre Dame, Indiana 46556

Library of Congress Catalog Card Number: 84-71674

International Standard Book Number: 0-87793-324-3

Photography:
    Bill Conyers, 62; Howard Johnson, 48; John Lanzone, front cover & 10; Joan Sauro, 16 & 30; Vernon Sigl, 78 & 84.

Cover Design: Thomas Ringenberg

Printed and bound in the United States of America.

To Jean, Kevin and Jan, with love

"Those who can sit in silence with their fellowman not knowing what to say but knowing that they should be there, can bring new life to a dying heart. Those who are not afraid to hold a hand in gratitude, to shed tears in grief, and to let a sigh of distress arise straight from the heart, can break through paralyzing boundaries and witness the birth of a new fellowship, the fellowship of the broken."

Henri J. M. Nouwen
Out of Solitude

Contents

Introduction

Calls for Our Love . . . and Questions!

One afternoon as I entered a nursing home for a pastoral visit I saw a 10-year-old boy seated next to a 90-year-old woman. The two held hands. Neither said a word. They simply sat and smiled.

The scene itself surprised me. The woman had no immediate family in the area. She frequently sat just inside the entry to the home and called out to any who came near, "Come here! Come here!" Nearly all passed her by, and on days when she was not seated near the door, cries would issue from her room, "Come here! Come here!" Now she gently caressed a young hand which held her own.

"Are you family?" I asked, as I took a place on the couch next to the two of them. The woman smiled at me, said nothing, and looked over at the boy.

"No," answered the boy, without a hint of self-consciousness. "I just came to find out some information for a school assignment. This nice woman kept saying, 'Come here.' I thought I'd better come."

After a few minutes I left the two, still holding hands. When I passed the couch an hour later the boy had gone, but the woman's face was peaceful. She looked alternately out the door and at her hand.

"Come here!" How many times and from how many different persons we can hear that call. Family members. Neighbors. Members of our church. We may sense the call from total strangers who live in loneliness and need the touch of friendship. The cries are not always so direct as "Come here!" or even "Please do visit me." Eyes give the message. So do the urgings we can feel within our own hearts. The calls for our love may come quietly, but still we hear them.

With the keen insight of childhood, that 10-year-old boy on the couch heard the call and responded. With the sensitivity of the young he freely gave the woman just what she needed. A hand. Time. Love. These were such direct and simple gifts.

For me, though, and perhaps for most of us, visiting has never come that easily. We hear the calls, but those calls are met by questions. We want to pay a visit, but how? We want to be of aid to a family member, but what in particular should we do? The questions take on specific forms according to the situations we are dealing with:

"Mrs. White is so confused. I want to visit her, but I just don't know what to do when I go in her room. Is there any way I can let her know that someone still cares?"

"Mr. Bitner is completely homebound now. He longs for the fellowship of the church. Isn't there some way we can help him be a part of what's going on?"

"Mother is going into Riverview next week. It's such a fine home. She has a wonderful attitude about this, but still I know it's hard for her. Is there anything I can do to help?"

"Our choir is going to sing at Crest Acres this Sunday afternoon. The residents always enjoy it when we come,

but I'm wondering if we could do
something a little extra this time which
might add meaning to our visit?"

As a pastor, I often have my own questions. I
know these too are shared by lay visitors and
family members. "How can I reach the deepest
needs of these people with the message of God's
love?" "What scripture texts are most appropriate
for bedside reading?" "Are there passages which
can be particularly helpful to the terminally ill
and to their families?"

In treating questions such as those just expressed I have chosen to start with what may appear to be the most heart-rending of areas. This
is the whole area of relating to persons who are
profoundly confused or have passed into a coma.
I have chosen this area as the place to start part-
ly because it may be of immediate and personal
concern to some who are reading these pages. I
have chosen it too because what we learn about
visiting under the most difficult circumstances
will illuminate the other areas of visiting we look
at as well.

The questions which assail many of us when
we go to pay a visit do have answers. Good
ones. Practical ones. More than any other persons, the men and women who have shared with
me the answers are the elderly themselves. They

have shared with their smiles and with their touch. They have taught with their words. They have spoken with their eyes. What I offer here, I offer in gratitude. My hope and my prayer is that the following pages may in some way aid you in your own ministry of love.

— Stephen V. Doughty

1.

When Someone Is Confused or in a Coma

Many of the visits we pay to the aged we can pay with joy and comfort. We enter a sparkling room. The person we wish to see greets us warmly. We laugh with that person, share news, trade our latest experiences and our thoughts. When it comes time for us to go, we know that our own lives have been enriched by the time we have spent. The look on the face of the one we have visited says the enrichment has been mutual. The visit has been what we hoped and prayed for.

At other times, however, the visit is not as easy. Someone we have known for years starts to drift and to repeat phrases, seems to have forgotten our last visit, or is not even sure who we are or why we have come. Is there any way we still can be of help to this person? Can we, with sensitivity, still express our friendship and our love?

Or again, someone we love lies in what the doctors have told us is a coma. The person does not seem aware of our presence at all. What then? Are there still ways to relate to this one we have cared for? Is there anything we should bear in mind? Are there steps we should follow?

In truth, with both the confused person and the person who lies in a coma, there are steps to take. Our efforts as a family member or parish visitor may touch the person deeply. To see how this is true, it will be helpful first to look at a few basic insights from the field of medicine.

Medical Insights on Confusion

Sister Yvette Mallow, a Benedictine nun, lives in the Black Hills of South Dakota. For many years she has served there as chaplain to nursing home residents and hospital patients from a wide variety of religious backgrounds. She echoes not only her own experience but also the broad opinion of the medical profession when she says, "It is terribly important that visitors not write the confused person off as a hopeless case. Recognizing that person's potential for understanding is the place to begin."

Potential is the key word. Through the middle years of this century all forms of confusion were regarded as largely the same. The confused person was labeled senile, and there was little expectation of improvement. The only changes expected were further decline, greater confusion, and finally, total withdrawal. In recent decades a more complex and hopeful picture of confusion has emerged.

There are basically two kinds of confusion: functional confusion and organic brain-syndrome confusion. Functional confusion comes about as a result of patient withdrawal. A person may have developed some disability, such as a hearing loss or speech impediment. The person may have suffered the loss of a loved one. Rather than struggle to adjust to the new situation, the person simply withdraws and lives in his or her own world.

Functional confusion may also result from a variety of short-term causes. Severe constipation can cause temporary confusion. For many elderly people night brings on confusion. Being tired sometimes plays a part. An exhausted patient may call Frank by the wrong name, knowing all the while it is Frank, but making the same mistake young parents often do when they confuse the names of their children. Too much medication or conflicting medications will produce confusion.

Functional confusion has a high potential for treatment. To this end, many nursing homes now employ the techniques of Reality Reorientation. This form of therapy involves letting the patient know his or her name, location, the time of day, and what the patient is capable of doing. Repetition of this basic information, plus attention to treatable medical problems and involving the person in appropriate activities, can draw the resident back into constructive forms of communication.

Organically related confusion is often irreversible and treatment is difficult. Organic confusion results from physical changes directly affecting the brain. These include hardening of the arteries, brain tumors, and brain damage caused by a severe blow to the head. Though the causes of organic confusion may well be irreversible, it is important for visitors to realize that even a brain-damaged accident victim may have moments of response and recognition. A stroke victim or a victim of brain cancer may have periods of greater clarity. I have on several occasions witnessed moments of very beautiful communication between family members and the victims of organically based confusion. A touch of the hand, a thank you, a look from the eyes can speak worlds, both to the visitors and to the one who is ill.

When visiting a person who is confused, the fundamental point is not to despair but rather to be honestly hopeful. Whether the person you visit is suffering from functional confusion or organic confusion, there is still the potential for sharing. As we shall see shortly, there are still ways you can relate positively, lovingly, and helpfully to that person's needs.

Medical Insights on a Coma

The person in a coma is in a far greater state of physical withdrawal than a person who is confused. The comatose person does not respond outwardly to light, sound or other stimuli, except perhaps by a slight turning of the head or other limited movement. Even though the person may make no outward signs of response, however, he or she may be keenly aware of what is going on in the room. When a person passes into a coma, the senses of hearing and touch are often the last to go. Indeed, many times these senses become heightened. Let me share with you just a few of many examples:

For two weeks I visited regularly a woman who became comatose following a reaction to new medication. She gave no signs of being aware that I was with her. When she came out of her coma she said, "I knew each time you were there. I could hear your words."

A teen-age boy lay in a coma for four months following an accident. "I felt like I was a prisoner in my body," he said after he recovered. He had known his doctors and recognized them when he came out of the coma, even though he had never met them before entering the hospital. The boy was aware of his visitors and what they had been saying.

An 82-year-old woman lapsed into a coma and did not speak for two weeks. One morning, as medical assistants were wheeling her back to her room following some tests, she spoke. It was clear from her words that she knew exactly where she was and where the medical assistants were taking her.

Often, of course, the person in a coma is not aware. Many who recover have no recollection of recent events. For others, we simply do not know. The important thing for visitors and family members to remember is that the comatose person *may* be keenly aware, even though he or she gives no outward sign.

Ten Helpful Points

"Well, all right," we may say to all of this, "but what can we *do*?" Building on this knowledge of the comatose and the confused, what steps should we be prepared to take? What should we bear in mind as we visit? Here are 10 points which can be of help to you and to the person you are visiting.

1. *When you enter the room, speak the person's name and let the person know who you are, where the person is, and what time of day it is.* You can do this simply and naturally:

"Hi, Jane. This is Pat. I've come to be with you at the nursing home this afternoon."

"Hello, Greg. This is Michelle. I just wanted to be with you at the hospital this morning."

These few expressions go a long way toward letting the confused or comatose person know what is going on. They are a far cry from the visitor who bursts in, slaps the person's hand, and asks, "Mama, do you recognize me? Mama, do you know who I am?" Mama may know perfectly well, but she also may be too weak to respond. *You* take the initiative. *You* reach out to the person. Doing this will help put the person at ease. You will also help that person understand what is going on.

2. *When you leave, let the person know that you are going.* Complete your visit as you would any other. The touch of a hand, a kiss, the simple words, "Goodbye, I'm going now," will help keep the person oriented. If you know when you will be back, say so. If not, just letting the person know you are going will help end the visit comfortably.

3. *Touching is important.* Taking a person's hand is a helpful, meaningful form of communication. Taking the hand of someone in a coma can reinforce the sense of your presence. To the comatose and the confused alike, the touch of a hand can come as a welcome sign of warmth and understanding.

4. *Silence can be golden.* You need not worry about silence. Often it is the best thing. Many times the most precious gift a person can receive is the knowledge that a loved one is sitting quietly by, still caring, still understanding, still loving.

One afternoon a friend of mine sat quietly in a chair next to a woman suffering from a brain tumor. My friend had gone to stay with her while the woman's husband went off for some needed rest of his own. Other than introducing herself, my friend said nothing. She knew conversation was an immense strain for the patient, and she simply sat by the woman's bed, holding her hand. After 20 minutes, the woman in the bed spoke her only words of the day. "Sally," she said, with great feeling, "you're so good to me."

Silence. Our quiet, caring presence with another. Often this is exactly what that other person needs.

5. *When you speak, speak so that the person can understand.* The point is obvious, but we may need to remind ourselves. Always speak slowly and distinctly. If the person has difficulty, repeat yourself. You may raise your voice, but try not to go to a higher pitch. The hard of hearing frequently have more difficulty with the higher tones. In times of stress our voices have a natural tendency to rise, so make a special effort to keep your words strong and clear without letting your voice go higher.

6. *If you don't want the person to hear something, leave the room.* This applies to the comatose patient, who may hear without giving any signs of awareness. It also applies to the confused person, who may well be comprehending

more than we realize.

One 94-year-old man who had been in a state of confusion for two years suddenly said to me, "They're electing a new governor today." He then named both of the candidates and the probable winner. He was right on all counts. After this he moved into a halting discussion of other political matters. No one had talked over any of this with him. He must have heard the conversations of aides going in and out of his room, or perhaps news reports from his roommate's radio. This was fine, but the incident serves as a reminder. Be sensitive in your talking. People often receive more than we think they do.

7. *Be willing to listen.* If a person wants to talk, the most important thing you can do is listen. This is particularly true if the person is expressing discouragement or frustration. At such a time what the person most needs is not advice, but someone who will listen to feelings which may have become bottled up and need an outlet.

If the person cannot talk, but is expressing an emotion through his or her eyes, or through facial expressions, follow carefully with your own eyes. You may then respond simply and sensitively:

"I'm glad to see you too, Tom."

"I know, darling. I'm sorry. I understand."

A person who feels another has listened no longer feels alone.

8. *Know that you can still show love.* When we are in the presence of someone who is comatose or confused, we may experience feelings of frustration. We may yearn to "do something more." We may wish to take away the illness, to enter into the old ways of communicating, to lift entirely the burden of suffering. All of these are natural and honest feelings.

And yet, if you are present with the person, if in simple ways you let the person know you are there and that you care, you are meeting that person's deepest needs. You are still expressing your love. Even though this may be a different form of expression from what you are used to, it is as deep and as important as any expression of love you have ever shared.

9. *Know that the person still has something to give to you.* Knowing that you can still show love is a vital part of your attitude as a visitor. The other part of your attitude, equally important, is knowing that the person you visit still has something to give to you.

In their book, *Aging—The Fulfillment of Life*, Henri Nouwen and Walter J. Gaffney constantly stress that if people are to give love to the aged, they must realize how much the aged can give to them. This surely holds true both for the confused person and for the person who lies deep in a coma. There is still something infinitely precious in that life. Cherish it.

10. *Frame your visits with prayer.* For many years, I have found rich blessings in taking time to pray before and after a period of visiting. Lay visitors to the sick and family members I talk to have expressed the same feelings regarding this great source of help.

Before you visit, ask God to guide you and increase your sensitivity to the one you are going to see. You may wish to ask that God help prepare the one you are visiting for the time which you will spend together. As you ask this, realize that God's preparations may take place deep within the other person. You may see no outward signs, but still the awareness and the receiving spirit can be there. Ask too that God will help you stay open to all that this person has to give to you.

When you are done, give thanks for the visit. Commit to God the time which you have shared together. Ask God to continue to use the moments of understanding you have given and received.

"I could never make my visits without the blessings God gives through prayer," a lay visitor once told me. The expression on her face told me she had received these blessings many times. She learned what we all can learn. Ask God's aid, and time and again God will enable us to pay those visits which we really cannot pay on our own. Return our thanks and ask God's blessing after the visit is done, and God will continue to use the love we sought to share.

Like so many of life's most important and loving acts, the above points are all quite simple. It is easy to forget them in the pressures of the moment, but do try to keep them in mind. I know that these small considerations can help turn even a hard time into one which is truly of eternal worth, both for you and for the one you are visiting.

2.

Adjustment and Ongoing Visits

"We're taking Dad over to a home next week. He doesn't know this yet, but the doctors just talked to us. He can't go back on his own when he gets out of the hospital, and he will be needing more care than we can give. What should we tell him?"

"This is such a big change for both of us. Frank and I have been together every day for 51 years. We've talked it over. We both know it would be better for him to go to Good Neighbors. We've decided on our own, but it's still going to be hard. Is there anything that can help Frank, and help me, as we go through this change?"

"Grandma smiles when she talks about going into the home, but I know that inside she is anxious. What can I do for her?"

Family members frequently ask questions such as these. Lay visitors, neighbors and clergy ask similar questions, wondering what they can do to help people adjust to new situations. And beyond the phase of adjustment, there arise the questions of ongoing care and visitation. How can we provide continued assurance? What special steps will put us in touch with the environment of the people we are visiting and with their deeper needs? If the one we care for lives at a distance, what can we do to extend our love and the sense of our presence?

All of these questions do have positive answers. Some of the answers are challenging. Application of them may take our patience, our prayers, our persistence. Still, in practical ways we can assist a person's adjustment and provide that needed sense of ongoing contact and love.

Feelings

Feelings are an important place to start. These include the feelings of the person whose life is changing. They also include the feelings of family members. Feelings stand forth as a particularly important factor during any adjustment period, but they may become vitally important at other times as well.

Some of these feelings are hard to get at. Some are negative, and perhaps even frightening. Yet it is only when family members and visitors recognize the feelings and deal constructively with them that positive adjustment to the situation can take place for everyone involved.

What feelings should we bear in mind? Here are some emotions which may arise in the person or in family members.

The person entering a home may have understandable feelings of *regret.* It is hard to leave a home or a neighborhood where one has lived for many years. The new nursing home resident may express these feelings openly or even angrily. Or the resident may quietly cope with these feelings, keeping them inside. In either case aching thoughts are often present. "I miss my home and I miss the tree outside my window."

The person entering a nursing home may need to cope with feelings of *fear.* "What are these people going to be like? How are they going to treat me?" The first weeks are often packed with new faces, different routines, and strange experiences. Just as in any other move from one location to another, it is natural for the new resident to have recurrent times of wondering, "Am I really going to be all right here?"

Loneliness is another emotion with which the person may contend. He or she may be wondering just when there will be a chance to see family and old friends. New relationships haven't formed. Withdrawal may set in. One woman I knew went through a period of deep loneliness during her first six weeks in an excellent home. Her family and the nursing home staff helped bring her through this. They gently encouraged her to enter into the activities of the home. Soon she was contributing daily to the lives of others and enjoying more friendships than she had in years. For this to have happened, though, the staff and her family needed to be aware of her initial feelings.

Family members also may need to cope with difficult feelings when a loved one enters a home. *"I wish I could do more"* is a frequent reaction. In our minds we may know the move is for the best. Our loved one will receive better care than we could ever provide on our own. Still, the desire to keep things the way they were continues. Adjusting to what we know is right may take time.

Children sometimes experience feelings of *guilt* when a parent enters a nursing home. They may wish to spare their parent the pain of change. They may be afraid that the parent will feel rejected by them. They may simply think that they have not done enough and that the whole situation could have been avoided.

Understanding emotions plays an important part in the successful adjustment to nursing home life. Emotions which are understood can be handled far more easily and constructively than those which are not. Beyond an understanding of human feelings, however, what steps can a person take? What might family members or other visitors do to ease a person's fears or loneliness? How is it possible to encourage a positive adjustment? And what practical measures can we take to provide continued care and support for someone in a home?

Eleven Basic Helps

Here are 11 points to bear in mind. I have found them helpful, and I know many others have found them helpful too.

1. *Know the facility.* Take the time to tour the home. This is important for family members and for all other regular visitors as well. Ask the director of the home to show you its resources—the dining area, any lounge areas, therapy centers, activity rooms, the layout of the

hallways. If you feel at home with the facility, this will come through in your visiting. You will relate more clearly to the daily experiences of the person you are visiting. And, with your awareness of the home you may be able to help entering residents feel more relaxed and comfortable in the new setting.

When someone is planning to enter a nursing home, friends or family members should arrange a tour for that person several days before he or she plans to take up residence. This will remove some of the strangeness and will help the person feel more at home when moving day comes.

2. *Be honest.* Sometimes a well-meaning family member will say, "We're just going to try this out for a little while, Dad," when this really isn't true. Such statements build false hopes. They can also lead to painful disillusionment. A delightful old man was informed by a family member that he was going to be put in the local hospital for a few days. It wasn't the hospital at all. It was a nursing home. When he found out where he was, he rebelled bitterly at having been treated like a child. The truth might have hurt, but it would not have hurt as much as the evasion.

Honesty is essential. It gives people the respect they deserve. It also maintains trust, and trust, especially in one's own family, plays a critical role during the period of adjustment.

3. *Talk with the activities director.* Nearly all nursing homes have a person in charge of activities such as games, crafts and educational events. Talk with this person. Learn what activities are available. Also, let the activities director know of any special skills or experiences which the person you are concerned for may have to offer. The director will be grateful for your interest and can be a source of continuing help.

4. *Let the person you are visiting express feelings.* If the one you are visiting is distressed, among the most loving things you can do is listen. Someone who is listened to will feel understood and loved. That is very strong support indeed, even when external circumstances cannot be changed.

For six weeks one resident I knew poured out his anger in the presence of his son and daughter-in-law. The couple made no promises of a change. They couldn't. All they could do was listen patiently and with understanding. In time the man's anger faded. He felt the love which had been present with him all along. He began to ask about his grandchildren and neighbors.

Listening will accomplish far more over the

long run than sharp comments such as, "Don't talk like that!" or "Don't say that!" Listen, and you will provide a pathway along which your friend or loved one can move back toward more positive feelings again.

A special word is in order here for close family members. As a member of the clergy, I have many times heard the comment, "He's nice when you're around, but when I'm alone with him, he's a different person!" Family members, particularly a husband or wife of many years, may be solitary witness to the greatest anger. This can be very hard to take. If you find yourself in this situation, do seek the support of your pastor, friends, or other family members. You should not have to bear the hurt alone. Just having someone else to talk to can release some of the pressure you feel. At the same time, know that in all likelihood your loved one is showing these emotions in your presence because he or she trusts you more than any other person. You have done nothing wrong. It is a measure of your closeness that you see the things you do.

5. *Express your own feelings too.* If you are wishing you could do more, if you hurt for the one you are with, do not be afraid to share such feelings. The person who says, "Fran, I'm *so* sorry about your fall," or "Dad, I wish it didn't

have to be this way," is communicating on a very deep level. You need not force such statements where they are not natural, but if you feel like sharing them, go ahead. The other person will understand the depth of your concern.

6. *Know the finances and be able to explain them clearly.* This is particularly important for family members, though lay visitors and clergy sometimes need to provide assurance in this area too. Many elderly persons experience financial worries when entering a home. Some find the finances confusing. Some fear they will be "put out" if their savings become exhausted. Frequently an older person regrets using funds which had been put aside as a gift for the next generation.

Talk to the director of the home about finances. Ask any questions you might have. Learn about Medicare provisions in the event of added illness. Get to know the details of coverage should a person's funds run out. Such a talk should reassure you. In turn, you will be able to reassure the one you are responsible to. If the person wishes a detailed explanation about some special points of concern, you will be able to provide it. Many times, however, all that the resident needs is the confident assurance of a family member or a close friend. "I talked to the director about finances, and everything is fine."

For family members, if your loved one appears upset over using funds that were intended for you, deal with the situation openly. A friend of mine visited an elderly woman one day and found her more relaxed than she had been in weeks. "My daughter talked with me about the money today," she said. She didn't elaborate. She didn't need to. My friend knew that the daughter had told her what she deserved to hear. Above all else, her children wanted to see her well cared for. With her love, she had given them far greater riches than any financial inheritance.

7. *Personalize the living space.* When someone is entering a home, encourage that person to choose a few special items to bring into the new setting—favorite photographs, knickknacks, a hand-made blanket, an old hat. Objects such as these can provide a feeling of familiarity. If, due to illness, the person cannot make a selection, seek out a few items yourself which you think will give a sense of home.

Church visitors can help maintain a homelike atmosphere. Bring a church bulletin when you visit, or a drawing by some children, or a photo of some friends at church. Such objects will brighten up the room as well as maintain contact with the larger church family.

8. *Let the person know your visiting plans.*
Tell the person when you plan to come back,
and keep that commitment. This is particularly
important for family members. Vague statements
of "I'll be back" and broken commitments increase loneliness. A definite statement of when
you plan to return gives the person something to
look forward to. This is true even if you live at a
distance and are not able to visit again for a
period of weeks or months.

If you live close at hand, a steady routine
may be helpful for you as well as for the person
you are reaching out to:

"I keep Tuesday nights clear. That's always
when I go see Mom."

"My son drives over here every Tuesday
night after work. I always know I'm going
to see him."

Routines help both ways. They spare visitors
that painful mixture of guilt and regret when suddenly they realize that more time has passed between visits than they intended. And routines
spare residents the sad experience of wondering
day after day when family members or church
visitors are going to come again.

If you find that you cannot come at a time
when you planned, make a phone call to let the

person know, and say when you will be over again. This will ease any worries the person might have relating to your absence. Your call will help the person feel cared for rather than abandoned.

9. *If you visit several persons regularly, keep notes.* This is a simple process. It takes only a little extra time, but can be a great help for lay or clergy visitors. Your notes should include the basic information which will help you relate personally to the people you are seeing. When are their birthdays? It is always nice to remember these occasions with a card. What are the names of other family members? Who are their physicians? Are there any particular health concerns? Where have they lived? What has been their work and what special skills or enjoyments does each one have?

You need not conduct a formal interview to gain the answers to such questions. The information will come out quite naturally during your first visits as you grow to know each other. Appendix I suggests a simple form for recording this basic information.

As you continue your visits, it will be helpful to keep track of any new matters which arise. If the person you are visiting expresses worry over a family member or excitement at the approach of a special event such as a wedding or a graduation, make a note of it. This will help plan your next visit. "Oh, yes. I do want to ask Rachael about her grandson's graduation."

The best time to take notes will be shortly after the visit while the experience is still fresh. Store your notes in individual folders or large envelopes, one for each person you are visiting. A quick look at this material before your next visit will refresh your thoughts, remind you of special concerns, and may help you be sensitive to any new matters the person wishes to share.

10. *Family members who live at a distance can still carry out many of the suggestions offered here.* I have seen family members visit shortly before or just after a loved one has entered a home and be of great help during that time. They have clarified finances, shared feelings, expressed love deeply. The promise of a definite return visit has offered hope and the assurance that family ties will continue. The prayers of a family member are no less effectual for being offered at a distance of a hundred or even a thousand miles. The practical acts of love are not confined to those close at hand.

In addition to the avenues of activity suggested here, however, one further avenue is open to family members who live far away: *Keep your letters, cards and pictures coming!* I have yet to see the person who grew weary of receiving mail. The latest drawing by a grandchild, photos of a family gathering, even the briefest notes sharing recent news are ever welcome. Often such remembrances will lift spirits far higher than the sender realizes, and for far longer too. Mail becomes a source of joyful conversations with visitors, staff members and other residents. Even the confused and those greatly weakened by illness will point with a smile to some new picture or message on their bedside table.

The best way to handle correspondence is to set aside a regular time for doing it. "I try to send something to Mother every Tuesday," a friend told me. I am sure that occasionally things came up and she was a day or two late in doing what she wanted to. I am also sure, though, that her mild self-discipline and her faithfulness in this matter brought great joy nearly every Thursday or Friday many miles away.

11. *Use the spiritual resources of the home and of your church.* What are the opportunities for worship at the home? Does your pastor visit? Does the home have a chaplain? Do laypeople from various churches call or conduct special programs of religious enrichment? The spiritual resources will vary from home to home. It is im-

portant to know these resources and to be able to share them. Many residents will come faithfully to the opportunities for study and worship in their nursing facility. This is true not only of residents who were active church members before entering the home, but also of residents who may have had little previous contact with a worshiping community. They come now to worship and to study because they discover such opportunities are meeting needs deep within them.

Family members and other visitors may feel the need for special support too. If you are distressed on behalf of the one you are visiting, if you have questions, do feel free to talk to the chaplain of the home or to your minister or priest. Conversations with a spiritual counselor may well ease the stressful emotions you are feeling. Such conversations can restore perspective, provide fresh insights, and renew you for the task at hand.

Mutual support is another major resource available to visitors. In some churches, visitors meet at the end of an afternoon of calling. In a brief and warm time of gathering they talk over their experiences, share friendship, and take part in a closing devotion. Appendix II provides a simple format, and suggestions, for such a time of sharing and prayer.

Family members can find equally nourishing sources of support. Friendship with other persons who visit regularly may provide just the right avenue for conversations and those needed times of sharing. Some family members arrange for regular consultations among themselves.

And then there is the most fundamental resource of all. Prayer. This includes our own personal prayers for those who reside in hospitals and nursing homes or are confined to their homes. It also, I believe, should include the prayers of the wider church. I have seen family members who requested the prayers of Christian friends when their loved one moved to a nursing home and was having a particularly difficult time. I have known those who pray daily for hospital and nursing home residents, shut-ins, and for the teams of church members who visit them. We need steady, continuing prayers in our churches for the sick, the confined, and those in nursing homes and hospitals and their families. Prayer needs to be the undergirding and the uplifting of all that we do.

These are all simple, practical steps. Most of us at some point in our lives will have an opportunity to take them. The opportunity may come in relation to friends, to our parents, or to our spouse. The opportunity may be upon us now. It may lie somewhere in the future. In either case, the steps will still be there. Taking them, we will find that the way is less rugged, more natural, and more nourished by feelings of closeness, both for us and for the one whom we wish to accompany along the path.

3.

Aids for Worship and Sharing God's Love

Many who visit hospitals or nursing homes or make home visits to the aged wrestle with the question of how to share the message of God's love. Lay visitors and family members may wonder, "Isn't there something special we can give? Might a particular verse of scripture, a prayer, or some quiet act of personal sharing touch the hurt and lift the spirits?" For clergy, the wondering frequently arises when it comes time to lead worship at a nearby nursing home. "What can I take to the people at Shady Brook tomorrow? What can possibly meet the great variety of needs which I know will be gathered there?" For lay persons and clergy alike these wonderings become especially acute when trying to relate to persons whose ability to receive any message appears to have become clouded. We want to share the word of God's love and care, but how?

Clergy, of course, have the privilege and calling to share the sacrament of holy communion. In nursing homes and hospitals this is done in a variety of manners, according to the needs of the residents and the shape of their own religious traditions. Beyond serving communion, however, there is a great deal which both laypeople and clergy can do.

Let me relate here an experience I had a number of years ago. It startled me at first. Then the experience began to teach me. Initially, it taught in the areas of leading worship and sharing the message of God's love with larger groups of nursing home residents. Quickly, though, I began to see that this experience had fully as much to teach about those special moments of personal sharing at a bedside in a nursing home resident's room or in the home of a shut-in.

An Experience and Its Lessons

When I first began to lead worship in nursing homes, I knew that I was working with persons from a broad range of religious backgrounds. In this setting I followed what appeared to be a sensible practice. I would take Sunday's sermon and then slightly reduce and rework it. On those days when I knew my most recent sermon would not do, I would simply reach back for an earlier sermon. In either case, I adopted a pattern of scripture reading followed by a 10-15 minute talk to the residents.

However, I soon noticed that these efforts produced the same general results time after time—low response and questionable communication. Once I had finished with the scripture reading, eyes tended to move about the room, minds obviously wandered, whole groups became distracted. I started to ask, "Could something work better than this?"

One day I got quite stuck. It was during Lent. Sunday morning's sermon in no way fit the needs of the people. Neither, it appeared, did anything else I looked at. "Ah," I thought half an hour before the service, "I'll just have to read the Suffering Servant passages from Isaiah and let it go at that!" *Just* read the Suffering Servant passages! As I read them that afternoon, eyes that usually wandered stayed fixed and distractions ceased. I shared a few simple comments. We prayed together. Glances after the service told me of a stronger response.

So I learned my first lesson: The careful

reading of a few familiar passages could create a degree of interest and a sense of community which my talks by themselves could not. Part of this, I am sure, sprang from the comfort and the steadiness of the familiar. A reading of the Twenty-third Psalm or 1 Corinthians 13 will awaken memories and draw residents into the experience of worship. For many, the reading will touch on cherished moments and precious learnings from long ago. The confused and the keen alike will attend to a carefully read passage of scripture.

Beyond the matter of familiarity, however, I am convinced that the strength of response to scripture reading resulted from the power inherent in the passages themselves. Jesus' parable of the Prodigal Son will always speak more directly, and touch more deeply, than any sermon I might offer on the subject of guilt and the mercies of God. The stark accounts of Jesus' passion and the sunburst passages telling his resurrection will forever communicate more perfectly than my own more extensive words about those same events.

The biblical word speaks freshly and with power. This is as true for those in nursing homes or hospitals as it is for any other gathering of people. It is true for those who have long been

familiar with that word and for those who are
just discovering its meaning for their lives. In
working with larger groups, I do share brief
thoughts introducing the passages I am going to
read. I do offer illustrations or personal incidents
relating to the passages. More and more, though,
I have learned to let the scriptures come forth
with their own freshness and power.

My experience pointed me first toward a
direct way of sharing God's message with larger
groups of residents. It has pointed me also to the
sharing of scripture in private visits as well. Like
many others who visit the elderly and long to
reach out to them, I had been searching for
something special to give. In time, I found that
something special had already been given:

"Could I share a reading with you before I
go?"

"Would you like to hear the Beatitudes?"

"The children made this copy of the Twenty-
third Psalm. Could we leave it here on your
table?"

Such questions invariably meet with a grateful
response.

There exists a variety of ways in which
scriptures can be shared. More on this will follow
shortly. For the moment, though, the essential

lesson I learned was just this: In the most personal visits, as well as in larger gatherings, a carefully selected passage of scripture will touch lives time and again with the restoring message of faith.

Special Passages

For a period of five years, while ministering in a nursing home near the parish I served, I kept careful track of the passages I shared with the residents and of their responses to these passages. What passages seemed most familiar? Where would I occasionally see lips moving, saying the words quietly as I read them aloud? I kept track too of biblical themes and events. What themes appeared to be bound up most tightly with the needs of the residents? What special events did the residents respond to and welcome as reflecting their own struggles? A gaze, a smile, a thoughtful silence, a handclasp—these often gave the answer. Some of the answers were easy to anticipate. Some surprised me. Let me share them with you here, together with a few brief comments.

1. *Themes of Special Interest*—Certain themes over the years have appeared to bring particular joy and response in the hearing. These are:

God's glory in creation. As much as any other persons, the elderly are deeply sensitive to the beauty with which God surrounds us. Favorite passages for treating this theme are Genesis 1:1-13 and 1:24-31, and Psalms 8, 19:1-6, and 23.

Taking part in God's mission. Older persons don't just hear about mission. Many take part in it significantly with their daily acts of kindness, their gifts, their prayers. Familiar passages reflecting their call are Matthew 5:13-16, 25:31-40, and 28:16-20.

The love we can share. Many residents are deeply sensitive to the need for showing compassion, not only to their roommates, to the sick, and to new residents, but also to the staff members who daily work around them. Two excellent passages for sharing this theme are 1 Corinthians 13 and 2 Corinthians 5:16-20.

God's love for us. Favorite passages here are from the gospel of John 3:16-17, 10:7-11, and Mark 10:13-16.

God's mercy for us. At first I was surprised at how intently some residents listened when I read passages telling of God's forgiveness. My own sins, I was sure, were greater than those who listened. Then I recalled how it is that every one of us stands in need of God's mercy. When we receive word of God's forgiveness, we listen. And we receive that word with great joy. Favorite passages for hearing that message are the three parables of lost things, Luke 15:1-7, 8-10, 11-32, and the story of the woman caught in adultery, John 8:1-11.

Comfort for our anxieties. This is far from the only theme needing to be shared with older friends, but it clearly is an important one for them, as it is for us all. Over the years I have found the following passages to be particularly helpful: Isaiah 40:28-31; Matthew 6:25-33 and 11:28-30; Romans 8:31-39; Philippians 4:4-9.

The Beatitudes. These simple verses announcing the theme of God's blessings appear always to reach a great variety of needs. Matthew 5:1-12.

2. *Events*—Four events, all of them from the gospels, generate particularly strong responses. These events are:

- The temptation of Jesus—Luke 4:1-13
- The call of the disciples—Matthew 4:18-22

- Mary and Martha—Luke 10:38-40
- The widow's mite—Luke 21:1-4

Each of these events provides a special point of contact for the listener. It is a comfort to know that Jesus struggled with fierce temptations, even as we do through all of our lives. We see the disciples leave their nets and follow him, and we know that in our lives we must continue to do the same. Mary and Martha frequently produce gentle smiles among listeners to their story, plus the inward recognition, "I need more stillness in my life. I need to pause again and simply receive what our Lord wishes to give." The account of the widow's mite imparts a strong word of hope to those who feel they are giving little when, in truth, they are giving everything in the service of his kingdom.

3. *Parables*—In addition to the parables of the lost sheep, the lost coin, and the lost son (Luke 15:1-7, 8-10, 11-32), the following parables appear to be particularly appropriate for oral reading:

- The Good Samaritan—Luke 10:25-37
- The Mustard Seed and the Leaven—Luke 13:18-21
- The Two Houses—Matthew 7:24-27
- The Sower—Matthew 13:1-8, 18-23

4. *Favorite Psalms*—The Book of Psalms contains many passages which ring with the familiar and sound the richest messages of faith. Among the favorites are Psalms 8, 19:1-6, 23, 46, 100, 121, and 139:1-12.

5. *Church Seasons*—The weeks preceding Christmas and Easter provide many opportunities for sharing the written word. Here are especially familiar passages:

- Advent and Christmas—Isaiah 9:2-7, Luke 1:26-38, 39-56, 2:1-20, Matthew 2:1-12
- Lent and Easter—A variety of passages and events here kindle interest. Jesus' work among us and his suffering: Isaiah 42:1-4 and 52:13—53:12. Jesus' entry into Jerusalem, the Last Supper, the Crucifixion: Matthew 21:1-11, 26:20-29, 30-46, 47-56, and Luke 23:32-49. The Resurrection: Matthew 28:1-10, Luke 24:1-11, and John 20:1-18

Suggestions for Sharing

Here are six ways to share the above gifts from scripture. You and other visitors may see more.

1. *Worship Services.* This is the most obvious context for offering passages of scripture, though by no means is it the only one. Laypeo-

ple, as well as clergy, can provide simple worship experiences open to persons from a wide variety of religious backgrounds. A service comprised of carefully read scriptures coupled with hymn singing and prayer will yield a rich experience of worship. In planning the service, select a few texts which focus on a given theme. You may wish to intersperse some of the texts mentioned here with others which you feel are appropriate to the message of the day.

I have always found it helpful to practice oral reading before I go into a service. This is true even if I have read the text aloud many times before. The moments given over to such practice open me once again to what the passages really are saying. Many times, too, I have felt such practice helped me become more aware of those to whom I would be reading.

How many passages should a person read during a service of worship? I have found that usually six passages, interspersed with brief comments, two or three hymns, and a time of prayer will provide a full service. A service lasts a maximum of 40 minutes, and generally not more than half an hour. This particular format avoids the problem of needlessly fatiguing some of the residents. At the same time it allows for strong content, participation, varied forms of religious expression, and a community experience.

2. *Bedside Reading.* Many persons have a bible right beside their bed, but are unable to read it because of failing eyesight or loss of strength in their arms. Others, able to read to themselves, are uncertain about where to turn in the bible. Still others can read to themselves and do, and yet they will welcome the sound of a friend reading cherished words.

During special seasons of the year, you may wish to share a passage appropriate to that season. At other times, reading a parable, a psalm, or words from the letters of Paul can be a blessing both to the person you are visiting and to you. It is helpful, of course, to have in mind what you might read before you begin your visit. It is wise also to remain sensitive to the needs of the person you are seeing. Sometimes you find that a person just needs to talk. On the whole, though, you will receive a glad response to your question, "Would you like me to read something from the bible before I go?"

3. *Enrichment of Group Programs.* Little children and youth choirs come to sing at nursing homes. So do adult groups. Some community groups lead sing-alongs on a regular basis. Caring persons of all ages give of their time to provide entertainment for nursing home residents. Such

programs bring joy. They share love with persons who often feel forgotten. They return gifts of time and talent to the very people who have poured forth those gifts for many years.

On occasion it is quite possible to enrich these programs in one more way. A member of your group can stand forth and say, "While we're here this afternoon, we'd just like to share this message with you too." The group member may then read one of the familiar texts. In the case of small children, the children together can recite one of the psalms, the Beatitudes, or some other passage which they have learned. Such an offering will lift up the message of love which lies at the heart of all such visits.

4. *Large-print Gifts.* The helpfulness of larger print has been known for many years. Churches need to take note of this in the remembrances which they send to the elderly. A card from a religious education class, a place mat, a greeting from the women's group, men's group, or the governing body of the church is always a welcome gift. When handmade, particularly by children, the lettering on such items should be in large print. Decorations on a card or place mat might include the words of a psalm or some other familiar text. Large-print scripture passages can accompany other cards and gifts from the

Thank
You
God

church as well. Clear, readable print will provide the recipient with an ongoing source of thought and reflection.

5. *Wall Posters.* This takes the large-print idea and expands it. Posters with the words from favorite passages make lovely wall hangings for rooms, hallways, and dining areas. Congregations can make a church project out of providing posters. Have a Family Meal and Poster Party! After the meal, divide the congregation into groups of five or six persons each. Adults and children of all ages will enjoy selecting the texts, doing the lettering, and decorating the posters.

Planners of the poster party will want to have plenty of materials on hand, including poster board, felt pens of different colors, and perhaps magazine pictures for decoration. Planners also might wish to provide participants with a list of texts from which to choose the message for their posters. When the posters are complete, let each group share what it has done. Close the party with a song of thanksgiving. Select a delegation, again of all ages, to take the posters to the nursing home residents and shut-ins.

6. *Bible Study.* Many people, lay as well as clergy, provide meaningful opportunities for bible study in nursing homes. Not all residents are able to take part, but for those who do the study

often becomes a rich element in their lives. Participation in the study of the scriptures can reinforce a resident's ties with the ongoing work of the church. Scripture studies offer a chance for fellowship and continued personal growth.

Just as in the congregational setting, bible studies can be carried out in two forms: continuous study or fixed-term. The continuous study is a regular meeting, usually weekly, with no set termination. Participants may come and go, but the study carries on as a regular opportunity for all who wish to attend. The advantages of a continuous study lie in the relationships which may develop among participants as well as in the knowledge and personal growth which can come through ongoing group study of the scriptures. The disadvantages are twofold. First, clergy and laypeople alike may have difficulty committing themselves to the leadership of an ongoing study. Second, residents themselves may be reluctant to become involved with a long-term commitment or may feel hesitant about joining an already established group.

A fixed-term study will last anywhere from three weeks to two months. The study may focus on passages related to a particular season, on a theme of special interest, or on favorite passages, such as selections from the teachings of Jesus or from the Book of Psalms. Laity and clergy often find it easier to commit themselves to the leadership of fixed-term studies. Many residents welcome such studies as a source of enrichment for special times of the year or as an opportunity to focus on matters of keen personal interest. When a study has ended, they begin to look forward to the next time one will be available.

Whether you select the fixed-term or the continuous study, be sure to coordinate your study carefully with the activities director of the home. This person can advise you as to the best time for holding the study. The activities director will also help get the word out to those persons who would most benefit from the opportunity you are providing.

The format for the study should be simple and relaxed. After a time of personal greetings, you may wish to open with a prayer, thanking God for this chance to share together and asking God's blessing on the special time that you will spend with each other. You can then read the passage for the day. Several persons will probably follow in their own bibles as you read. Others will just listen. If you or your church can provide large-print editions of the bible, these will certainly be a help to some of the participants. When you have finished reading, be prepared to give a few introductory reflections. What does the passage mean to you personally? Where did you first hear it? Does it remind you of any events you have experienced or of any persons you have encountered? The residents will be interested in your sharing.

You may then ask a few questions which encourage the residents to share their own thoughts. How do they feel about the passage? What does it mean to them? Does it remind them of anything special that has happened in their lives? Does the passage seem to have a message for the people in the nursing home? For the church right now? For the world? Allow people time to reflect on your questions. As in all studies, some participants will begin to respond more readily than others, but the quiet ones surely will be receiving and reflecting too.

It is well to close the study time with prayer. Give thanks for the time you have had together and for thoughts which have been shared. You may wish to ask God's help in fulfilling the insights of the day. If any particular concerns have surfaced, offer these in prayer too. As the people leave, thank them for coming. It is a good idea also to let them know the passage you will be studying next time you are together.

A study should last about 40 minutes. Some

residents are able to study longer than that, but others are not. It is no kindness to send people away tired when they came to be refreshed. Some studies, too, may be over sooner than you thought. Don't worry if this happens. A time which is hallowed by prayer, by hearing the scriptures, and by the sharing of personal concerns is a great blessing, even if that time seems short to us.

Other Ways to Share Your Presence

In addition to the above suggestions, there are a number of other ways to reach out personally to the aged and the confined and to involve them actively in the ongoing life of your congregation. The following simple suggestions can be applied in a variety of situations.

1. *Make tapes and share them.* Many of those who are unable to attend worship services still long to be a part of the worshiping body they took part in for so many years. They miss the readings, the anthems, and the prayers which have nourished them. In recent years cassette recorders have provided a fitting way to meet their need.

Cassette recorders are inexpensive and easy to operate. Many churches will purchase two or more, one to be kept near the front of the sanctuary for recording all services, the others to be made available to shut-ins or to parish visitors as they pay their calls. Usually a member of the congregation will accept responsibility for cataloguing the tapes and changing them each week. To keep costs low and circulation high, many churches record over old services after the tapes have been in circulation for eight to 10 weeks.

Many times shut-ins would prefer to have visitors operate the cassette player for them. I knew a woman who received with great joy a tape of Sunday's service. She also received instructions on how to use the cassette player, which was then left for her to use whenever she wished. Two weeks later the visitors returned. The tape had not been played. The woman expressed real anxiety at the thought of damaging the tape.

The visitors and I learned from the experience. From then on the visitors took the initiative in playing the tapes, or portions of them, for the woman. In my own visits I would frequently hear her say, "It was so good to join in last Sunday's service," or "I *loved* hearing the children sing!"

2. *Involve the aged and the confined in the works of intercessory prayer.* Elderly persons and

shut-ins have a rich part to play in the ministry of prayer. And prayers by them are surely as important as prayers for them.

There are several ways to encourage participation in the works of prayer. If your church has a prayer chain, invite hospital patients, nursing home residents and shut-ins to share in its ongoing ministry. Some, of course, will feel more comfortable doing this than others; your invitation should give them complete freedom to respond as they wish. For those who do wish to take part, a member of the chain should be assigned to contact them regularly with all special prayer requests.

If prayer concerns are expressed at a woman's group or men's group, one member of the organization can be given responsibility for sharing those concerns with any shut-ins who desire to be kept informed. Similarly, if special prayers are offered during worship, a visitor can take responsibility for conveying these concerns to shut-ins, hospital patients or nursing home residents.

Over the years I have known a number of persons who had rich ministries of prayer from the confines of their room. For them, the weekly contact with other people's needs, the telephone call bringing a special prayer request, the visitor letting them know of someone else's concern all served to involve them in the life of the church at its very center. In turn, through their steady work, these persons have been a blessing to many.

3. *Bring children!* For shorter visits particularly, the bouncing form of a small child will bring more joy, and will leave more lasting memories, than any words we adults might ever speak. When an adult visitor passes along a nursing home corridor, a few heads may turn. When a child races along that same pathway, grins will break out from one end of the corridor to the other. When Christmas carolers pack into the home of a shut-in, their songs will lift the heart. After they are gone, though, the one they sang to may speak most often of "that cute little Johnson boy who couldn't hold still for two seconds!"

4. *Hold meetings in the homes of shut-ins.* This may sound unusual at first, but it can be a beautiful way to enrich contact with shut-ins and to utilize their skills. Many persons who are confined will welcome the chance to have a smaller group meet at the place where they live, particularly if assistance is provided with refreshments and any other needed arrangements. These persons will often have insights which the

rest of the church needs to hear.

One committee I knew was hosted for its meetings by a devoted and gracious couple. She had been confined to her bed for a number of years. The meetings provided an opportunity for warm fellowship and visiting. They also provided a chance for the entire congregation to benefit from what that good couple had to share.

Small parties too can be held at the residence of shut-ins. One active choir member invited the rest of the choir back to her home after an evening of Christmas caroling. Her husband had been confined there for some months. Several members of the choir helped her in providing light refreshments. The party gave her husband and the choir members an opportunity to enjoy one another's presence and to renew the bonds they had shared for many years.

5. *Involve new members in visiting.* Visitation is often carried out by old friends. It is the neighbor of 10 or 20 years who says, "I'll go see Alice in the nursing home." It is the middle-aged member, who has befriended another and watched that one grow old, who now says, "I'll stop by and see George." This is fitting. And older people deeply appreciate contact with those whom they have known for many years. In our visiting we need to celebrate and cherish the long-lasting ties.

At the same time, people who are confined and newer church members can benefit from meeting one another. Several years ago a young woman who recently moved to our area accompanied a long-term member on an afternoon of visitation. When it was over, the newer member said the visiting had been a wonderful experience. "I met such grand people, and now I'll be able to see the faces of people we pray for on Sunday." A week later I had a woman confined by illness say, "It was so good to meet that young woman from the church. I had heard about her, but had no idea who she was. Now I'm beginning to know her."

Involving newer members of the congregation in visiting helps prevent the aged or confined from feeling "I know so few of the people at our church anymore." It expands relationships in the context of Christian caring. It lets shut-ins and newcomers alike share their gifts of personality and love.

Passages for Days of Special Need

Several years ago a devout man in the church I was serving received word that his cancer, long in remission, had become active again. As we visited one afternoon he raised a concern which obviously weighed on his mind.

"I'm not afraid," he said. "I know what's happening, and I don't think it will be long. God has been good to me all these years, and I know God will be good to me now. I do, though, want to know of some passages I could turn to. I just want to be able to read a little each day. Could you suggest some verses to me?"

My friend's question was as beautiful for its openness as it was for the faith-filled desire he expressed. The question he asked arises in many different ways. It arises for the ill, who encounter it in the midst of their own need. It arises for clergy and lay visitors, who wonder what verses will most fully sustain the one they are concerned for. Family members often experience the same wondering. They experience it not only for the person who is ill, but for themselves as well. Family members too need the enriching words of hope and comfort.

I believe the following twenty passages are particularly helpful in life's seasons of special need. Some of them have been listed previously here for different uses. Others are listed for the first time. All of them can bring comfort to the ill, to their families, and to those who reach out to them. You may wish to read one or another of these during a visit. You may wish to turn to them for yourself. As you search them and listen to what they say, you may find one which you wish to pass on with a card or a letter. The ways of sharing will vary. The messages expressed in these verses are meant for us all.

- Psalms 23, 27:1-6, 46, 84, 121, 139:1-12
- Matthew 5:1-12, 11:28-30
- John 3:16-17, 14:1-4
- Romans 8:14-18, 28-39
- 1 Corinthians 13, 15:3-8, 15:35-58
- 2 Corinthians 4:16-18
- Philippians 1:19-22, 4:4-7, 4:8-9
- Revelation 21:1-4

On Offering Prayer

For lay visitors and clergy, praying with an elderly person can be a special way of sharing together in the gifts of faith. I can also attest that for those of us who are called upon to do the praying, the experience can be a bit frightening! Clergy are supposed to be professionals at such efforts, but I know that for myself I continue to approach the opportunity for prayer with inner searching. What should I offer in prayer? What can I lift in prayer which will express the needs this person feels? What will most honestly celebrate the bonds we hold in common? The same questions press themselves upon lay visitors.

Over the years it is the elderly themselves, and the Spirit working through them, who have taught me how to pray at the bedside and in the resident's room. How should one pray? The answer is ever the same. Pray simply. Pray directly. And pray in the words of the heart:

"Lord, we have this need, and we share it with you. . . ."

"We're concerned about these others, and now we ask that you will be with them. . . ."

"Dear God, we thank you for your love for us, and for the friendship we're able to rejoice in together."

Your words need not be long or eloquent. God will know all that you feel. So will the person with whom you are praying.

For what should you pray? Be sensitive during your visit, and ask for guidance. The themes will become clear. You may feel a need to join the person in prayer for his or her family. You may wish to give thanks for goodness in the life of the person you are visiting, or to pray for the easing of some discomfort in mind or body. You may sense the need to pray for others, for residents or for members of the staff. You may be led to give thanks for the ties you feel with the one you are visiting. If the person has offered some particular concern, you will want to include that in your prayer.

Rather than just announce you are going to pray, it is always wiser to ask. "Would you like me to pray with you before I go?" or "Could I offer a prayer?" A simple question such as either of these will provide a natural entry into the time of prayer. It will give the person you are visiting a chance to participate honestly in this act of worship. In 15 years I have only twice had persons say, "No, I'd rather not." In both cases, however, it was vitally important that the person was given the freedom to make that response. If someone says no to you, you accept that response in the same spirit of honesty and love as you would accept any other. In the vast majority of instances, though, you will find that your invitation to pray will be received with gratitude. So will any simple and genuine prayer that you offer. Through your prayer you will share deeply with the one you came to see.

4.

A Closing Word: Thank You to All Who Give the Time

Late one Friday afternoon I stopped off at a nursing home to look in on a friend who had resided there for more than three years. I made my way down one of the corridors, already warm with the aroma of a well-prepared chicken dinner, turned into my friend's room, and found her sound asleep on her bed. Nearly three years before she had issued firm instructions: "If you ever find me asleep, for heaven's sake, wake me up!"

Without such instructions I wouldn't have done what I did. As it was, though, I followed a procedure which I had used on a number of previous occasions. I touched her arm gently and spoke her name. She was well under and gave no response. I tried again, speaking her name a little louder. Still no response. I tried one last time, louder still. She awoke with a "Whoop!" which startled both of us. When we finished laughing, she dangled her frail legs over the side of her bed and looked right at me.

"I had the most wonderful time last week," she said, moving quickly to something which was still very much on her mind. "Two people from the church came to see me. We just talked and talked. It was so good to be with them." For a moment she strained to remember just who those two people were. She was sorry, she couldn't right now. "But," she added, relaxing and smiling again, "it was a beautiful time."

I knew several things about the two who had been to visit, and reflected on both of them after I left the nursing home that night. Each of them was a busy person, as busy with family concerns and community responsibilities as any other persons in the parish I was serving. Each too, I knew, had expressed some nervousness at the thought of visiting. They wondered about their sensitivity and skills. Could they really accomplish anything? "Might we make things worse?" I also knew that the two visitors had paid several other calls that same afternoon. I was absolutely certain that their visits had brought joy to those other lonely people too. The time these two persons gave had been wonderfully spent.

Visiting does take time. There is no question about it. Visiting also takes our willingness to become open to the needs of another. It takes our spiritual preparation. On many occasions, it takes continued reflection after the visit is done. All of this is true. Sometimes the fruits of visiting are obvious. "Thank you for coming. It was such a joy to have you." At other times the fruits are as quiet as a clasp of the hand or the knowledge that you have helped someone pour forth a hurt. At times the fruits are subtler still. You simply sit with the one you have come to see. When your visit is done, you know that in some special way, in the providence of God's care, the two of you have truly been together in the midst of your common need and your love.

Our emotions may cause us to cast about for other things to do. Our schedules can make the task of visiting seem impossible. And yet, in our inmost selves, we know otherwise. Together with our faith, God has given us no more precious gift than the gift of one another. There is no richer use of our time than to celebrate the bonds we share.

To you who are willing to take the time, to visit, to be present with another, thank you for what you are giving. Yours is a very precious gift.

Appendix I

BASIC INFORMATION SHEET

Name:_____

Birthday:_____

Address:_____

_____

Family members:_____

_____

Physicians:_____

_____

Health concerns:_____

_____

Places lived over the years:_____

_____

Work, hobbies, skills, interests:_____

_____

Other helpful information:_____

_____

_____

Visitors may add other sheets to record the dates of visits and any concerns to be kept in mind from one visit to the next.

Appendix II

A Service of Prayer and Sharing for Parish Visitors

Many who visit shut-ins, the hospitalized, and nursing home residents find it helpful to gather together and share a brief time of fellowship and devotion after their visiting is over. Here is a simple service which may be used or adapted for such occasions. Leadership of the service can be rotated among members of the group from one time to the next.

An Invitation to Worship
  —By the leader

Good friends, we have had the privilege of sharing in the ministry of God's love. We have sought to convey a blessing, and we have been blessed. We have wished to touch others, and they have touched us. Let us now, with thankful hearts and open minds, wait on the Everlasting One who loves us all.

A Prayer of Invocation
—In unison or by the leader

O Loving Lord God, we thank you for the privilege we have had in visiting. We thank you for concerns that have come to us, new insights that have lifted us, and any thoughts or questions which now stretch us. In this time of gathering may your Spirit work among us. Help us to share simply and openly with one another. And help us to listen attentively. Make us sensitive, Lord, for it is both as we share and as we listen that we can, together, grow in your ways of service and love. In the name of Jesus Christ our Savior. Amen.

A Time for Sharing

—Allow five to ten minutes for sharing among the group members. The purpose here is to let the visitors hear one another's joys, learnings or concerns. The leader may use one of the following suggestions to initiate the sharing:

> • Invite each visitor to name the persons he or she visited and to comment on how each person seemed to respond to being called upon.

• Ask each visitor to think in silence on this question: What were you most thankful for in each of the persons you visited today? Then go around the group, having all share their points of thankfulness.

• Ask the group: Did you learn anything new today about the skills and sensitivities of visiting?

• Ask each person to share a special joy and also a special concern from the visiting experience.

• Did anyone encounter a situation about which he or she would like the advice or insights of the group?

• What new insights into life, or into yourself, did you receive from the people you visited today?

It is always well to end the time of sharing with two further questions for the group:

• Did anyone encounter a situation of which future visitors should be made aware?

• Are there any special prayer concerns which have arisen out of the visiting?

A Time of Prayer

Intercessions—The leader may invite those present to pray in silence for the people they have visited, and then may wish to offer one of the following prayers of intercession:

O Loving and Everlasting God, we do lift before you these your children: (*mention the names of those visited*). We ask that you bless each of them according to your most perfect will. As we ourselves have been enriched by this chance to be with them, may they now be lifted by the knowledge of how special they are. Grant them the joy of knowing that they are continuing to give, and that their needs, their sensitivities, their insights are precious to others, as surely they are to you. And we ask that by the working of your Spirit they may continue to grow in the peace and wholeness which you alone can give.

or

O Eternal God, you who are the source of all our strength and can grant assurance in those places no human voice can reach, we pray for the easing of any distress we have seen today. Complete the intentions of our hearts by the action of your Spirit. In any spots of loneliness, may there now be thoughts of friendship and the knowledge of your ever-present love. In any places of fear or bewilderment, may there now come the blessings of your peace. In any places of sorrow, may there dawn a vision of the life and love which shall not end. These things we ask, Lord, that your assurance will grow in the lives of all whom we have seen.

or

Almighty God, you who have formed us to support one another as we journey through life, we pray for all those we have seen today. And we pray not only for them; we pray also for their families and all others who care for them. May these persons know that their gestures of love are not in vain, but rather are a part of your eternal works of love. When they grow fatigued, may they find in you their strength. When they are saddened, may they know your comfort. When joy sweeps upon them, may it nourish both them and the one they care for. And wherever there is an opening, Lord, may we show them the support and the friendship they need.

Thanksgivings—The leader may offer one of the following prayers of thanksgiving:

We thank you, Lord, for all that we have seen today. We thank you for love that has sparkled in the eyes of the aged and for courage that has glowed softly, unmistakably, even through the darkest hurt. We thank you for wisdom that has come with the years and for the gentle humor of those who have looked on life and seen it whole. Above all, Lord, we thank you for showing us that every life is precious and is to be cherished as a gift from you.

or

O Eternal and Living God, you who formed us so that learning and growth are ever to be a part of our lives, we thank you for stretching us today. Even for moments of nervousness, even for questions which still sound within our minds, we thank you. These are the expanders of the spirit. We know we need them. And we have needed too, Lord, a vision of other people's hurts, of their strengths, their endurance, and their capacity for love. You have given us, in one brief time, a chance to see all this. It has been a privilege beyond anything we deserve. We praise you for what you have given. May we now hold close everything that churns within our minds. And may we continue to grow.

or

O most gracious God, you who have called us to be Christians in fellowship with one another and with you, we thank you for all support we receive in our common task. We thank you for insights gleaned from one another's experience, for words of encouragement, and for the freedom to share our wonderings as well as our joys. And most fully, Lord, we celebrate your goodness toward us, in supporting us and sustaining us in all the tasks you call us to.

A Closing Prayer for God's Blessing—The following prayer, said by the leader or by the group in unison, may conclude the time of prayer:

O Loving Lord God, we thank you for the privilege you have given us today. What we have done has been imperfect. Our offering of self has been incomplete. And yet we know that you can take even the humblest gifts and turn them into something beautiful. We ask that you will receive all we have offered and use it according to your will. Bless those we have seen. And work within us, Lord, so that more and more fully we may serve your ministry of love.

In Jesus' name we pray. Amen.

Dismissal
—By the leader

And now let us go in peace. May we be sensitive to all in need. May we rejoice in the leading of the Spirit. May we serve the Living God in all that we do.

Amen.

Appendix III

Selected Bibliography of Resources

For Understanding Emotional and Physical Needs

> *Growing Older*, Margaret Hellie Huyck; Prentice Hall.
>
> *Ministry to the Sick*, Gerald R. Niklas and Charlotte Stefanics; Alba House.
>
> *The Church and the Older Person*, Robert M. Gray and David O. Moberg; Eerdmans.

Prayer and Devotional Resources

> *Be With Me, Lord: Prayers for the Sick*, Rodney DeMartini, S.M.; Ave Maria Press.

I Can Still Pray, C. W. and A. B.
Peckham; Parthenon Press.

Looking Down From Above, William A.
Lauterbach; Concordia Publishing
House.

Your Words in Prayer in Time of Illness,
Arnaldo Pangrazzi; Alba House.

General Resources for Ministry

Care and Counseling of the Aging,
William M. Clements; Fortress Press.

*Ministering to the Aging: Every Christian's
Call*, Rev. Bartholomew Laurello;
Paulist Press.

The Ministry of Listening, Donald Peel;
Seabury Press.

*Together by Your Side: A Book for
Comforting the Sick and Dying*, Rev.
Joseph M. Champlin; Ave Maria
Press.

Tape Resources for Ministry

Together by Your Side, Rev. Joseph M.
Champlin; a three-cassette series for
training the laity in visiting and
comforting; Ave Maria Press.

Aging and Ministry, Henri J. M.
     Nouwen; a two-cassette series; Ave
     Maria Press.

Photographic Essay and Text

Aging: The Fulfillment of Life, Henri J. M.
     Nouwen and Walter Gaffney;
     Doubleday.

Large-print Bibles

Good News Bible (extra-large type),
     American Bible Society.

New American Bible (giant print), Our
     Sunday Visitor.